D1636999

With appreciation

to

Gloria

from

Tina

date

_9/28/11_

The Fabric of friendship

Harold Shaw Publishers
Wheaton, Illinois

Cover and inside design by David LaPlaca

Compiled by Lil Copan

ISBN 0-87788-242-8

Library of Congress Cataloging-in-Publication Data applied for.

02   01   00   99   98   97   96

10   9   8   7   6   5   4   3   2   1

Contents

1 The Fabric of Friendship   7

2 The Language of Friendship   31

3 The Shelter of Friendship   55

4 The Grace of Friendship   77

1

The Fabric of Friendship

One of the earliest Bible stories is a friendship story. In a marvelous creative splurge, God made a universe, and in that universe, Adam and Eve. These first human beings were made for friendship with God and for relationship with each other. Thus, a circle of friends was begun.

From the familiar Bible stories to our present friendships, the fabric of friendship appears to be woven together with the same threads: kindness, sacrifice, patience, gentleness, and hospitality.

Constant use had not worn ragged the fabric of their friendship.
Dorothy Parker, The Standard of Living

Friendship is a special kind of loving.
Luci Shaw, "The Meaning of Friendship," Radix

True friendship is possible only when we recognize and accept the differences which distinguish rather than separate us from others.
Ignace Lepp, The Ways of Friendship

True friendship is a brotherhood of thought,
Knowing no selfishness—'twixt heart and heart,
Counting each friendly sacrifice as naught,
Finding content in having done its part.
Elton D. Spink, "True Friendship"

George never said "I told you so." Because that's not what friends are for.
James Marshall, George and Martha: Encore

An unusual—to me—a perfectly new character I suspected was yours: I desired to search it deeper, and know it better. . . . It was astonishing to see how quickly a certain pleasant ease tranquillized your manner: snarl as I would, you showed no surprise, fear, annoyance, or displeasure at my moroseness; you watched me, and now and then smiled at me with a simple yet sagacious grace I cannot describe. I was at once contented. . . .

Mr. Rochester to Jane Eyre in Charlotte Brontë's Jane Eyre

A loving heart carries with it, under every parallel of latitude, the warmth and light of the tropics. It plants its Eden in the wilderness and solitary place, and sows with flowers the gray desolation of roots and mosses.

John Greenleaf Whittier

If I can stop one heart from breaking,
I shall not live in vain;
If I can ease one life the aching,
Or cool one pain,
Or help one fainting robin

Unto his nest again,
I shall not live in vain.
Emily Dickinson

To love is to be vulnerable. Love anything, and your heart will
certainly be wrung and possibly broken.
C. S. Lewis

The best people possess a feeling for beauty, the courage to take risks, the
discipline to tell the truth, the capacity for sacrifice. Ironically, their virtue
makes them vulnerable; they are often wounded, sometimes destroyed.
Ernest Hemingway, A Farewell to Arms

One can give nothing whatever without giving oneself—that is to say,
risking oneself. If one cannot risk oneself, then one is simply
incapable of giving.
James Baldwin, The Fire Next Time

If you stop to be kind you must swerve often from your path.
Mary Webb

The holy passion of Friendship is of so sweet and steady and loyal and enduring a nature that it will last through a whole life-time, if not asked to lend money.

Mark Twain, Pudd'nhead Wilson

Long ago I made up my mind to let my friends have their peculiarities.

David Grayson

See everything; overlook a great deal; correct a little.

Pope John XXIII

You can give without loving, but you cannot love without giving.

Amy Carmichael

It is the steady and merciless increase of occupations, the augmented speed at which we are always trying to live, the crowding of each day with more work that it can profitably hold, which has cost us, among other good things, the undisturbed enjoyment of friends. Friendship takes time, and we have no time to give it.

Agnes Repplier, In the Dozy Hours

Have friends, not for the sake of receiving, but of giving.
Joseph Roux, Meditations of a Parish Priest

It is not a matter of thinking a great deal but of loving a great deal.
St. Teresa of Avila, The Interior Castle

The finest friendships have been formed in mutual adversity, as iron is most strongly united by the fiercest flame.
Charles C. Colton

As iron sharpens iron, so one man sharpens another.
Proverbs 26:17

Who is mighty? He who turns an enemy into a friend.
Talmud

Friendship is a spiritual thing. It is independent of matter or space or time. That which I love in my friend is not that which I see. What influences me in my friend is not his body, but his spirit.
John Drummond

We can have no relationship of depth or authenticity if we insist there is nothing wrong with us, or that it is always the other person's fault. . . . To refuse to take responsibility and admit our flaws makes the intimacy and love we seek in our relationships an impossibility.

Rebecca Manley Pippert

You can have a relationship without commitment but you can't really have friendship or love without commitment.

Madeleine L'Engle, "The Meaning of Friendship," Radix

Insomuch as any one pushes you nearer to God, he or she is your friend.

Anonymous

We must all learn to live together as brothers. Or we will all perish as fools.

Martin Luther King, Jr.

What I kept, I lost; what I spent, I had; what I gave, I have.

Persian proverb

Any deep relationship to another human being requires watchfulness and nourishment; otherwise, it is taken from us. And we cannot recapture it. This is a form of having and not having that is the root of innumerable tragedies.

Paul Tillich

Love takes off the mask we fear we cannot live with and know we cannot live without.

Robert Slater

Love is like the wild rose-briar;
Friendship like the holly-tree.
The holly is dark when the rose-briar blooms,
But which will bloom most constantly?

Emily Brontë, "Love and Friendship"

Friends are people you make part of your life just because you feel like it.

Frederick Buechner, Whistling in the Dark

We like someone because. We love someone although.
Henri De Montherlant

Our loyalty to one another sticks like love.
Robert Lowell

My friends were poor but honest.
William Shakespeare, All's Well That Ends Well

Friendship takes fear from the heart.
Mahabharata

When three of Job's friends heard of all the tragedy that had befallen him, they got in touch with each other and traveled from their homes to comfort and console him.
Job 2:11, TLB

Alone we can do so little; together we can do so much.
Helen Keller

A friend is the one who comes in when the whole world has gone out.
Anonymous

"I'm not coming, and that's flat." [said the Rat]. "And I *am* going to stick to my old river, *and* live in a hole, *and* boat, as I've always done. And what's more, Mole's going to stick to me and do as I do, aren't you Mole?"

"Of course I am," said the Mole loyally. "I'll always stick to you, Rat, and what you say is to be—has got to be. All the same, it sounds as if it might have been—well, rather fun, you know!" he added wistfully.
Kenneth Grahame, The Wind in the Willows

Every man should keep a fair-sized cemetery in which to bury the faults of his friends.
Henry Ward Beecher

Friendship . . . is a union of spirits, a marriage of hearts, and the bond thereto virtue.
William Penn, Fruits of Solitude

Friendship cannot live with ceremony, nor without civility.
Proverb

Let us not underestimate how hard it is to be compassionate. Compassion is hard because it requires the inner disposition to go with others to the place where they are weak, vulnerable, lonely, and broken.
Henri J. M. Nouwen

How to find friends and keep them? How to love them and grow with them? How to be friends in spite of differences in values and personalities and without limiting the other person's freedom? That's the challenge.
Muriel James and Louis M. Savary, The Heart of Friendship

The new friendship flourished like grass in spring. Everyone liked Laurie, and he privately informed his tutor that the Marches were "regularly splendid girls." With the delightful enthusiasm of youth, they took the solitary boy into their midst, and made much of him, and he found something very charming in the innocent companionship of these simple hearted girls. . . . He was quick to feel the influences they brought about him; and their busy, lively ways made him ashamed of the indolent life he led. . . .

Laurie was always playing truant, and running over to the Marches'. . . . What good times they had, to be sure! Such plays and tableaux, such sleigh rides and skating frolics, such pleasant evenings in the old parlor, and now and then such gay little parties at the great house.
Louisa May Alcott, Little Women

I cherish friendships with people whose daily work I do not begin to understand. They are insurance salespersons, accountants, coaches. We courteously ask each other how the work is going, but thirty seconds of reply settles that. Then we talk about what brings us together: old memories. The experience of having lived near each other. The way we were brought up as children. Where we are vacationing.
Martin E. Marty, Friendship

The most depressing part of the friendship game is that one can lose. . . . On the other hand, if we are not willing to run risks we are certainly never going to have friendships. Friendships can only occur . . . when we offer ourself to the other, and to offer ourself to

someone else is the most risky of all human endeavors.
Andrew M. Greeley, The Friendship Game

On my way back I met a little girl with a pitcher in her hand. We both stopped, and with the instinctive, unconventional camaraderie of childhood plunged into an intimate, confidential conversation. She was a jolly little soul, with black eyes and two long braids of black hair. We told each other how old we were, and how many dolls we had, and almost everything else there was to tell except our names which neither of us thought about. When we parted, I felt as though I were leaving a lifelong friend.
Lucy Maud Montgomery, The Alpine Path

Happiness is a sunbeam which may pass through a thousand bosoms without losing a particle of its original ray; nay, when it strikes on a kindred heart, like the converged light on a mirror, it reflects itself with redoubled brightness.—It is not perfected till it is shared.
Jane Porter

"Wery glad to see you, indeed, and hope our acquaintance may be a

long 'un, as the gen'l'm'n said to the fi' pun' note."
Charles Dickens, Pickwick Papers

There is no friend like the old friend, who has shared our morning days,
No greeting like his welcome, no homage like his praise:
Fame is the scentless sunflower, with gaudy crown of gold;
But friendship is the breathing rose, with sweets in every fold.
Oliver Wendell Holmes

A, B, C, and D,
Pray, playmates, agree.
E, F, and G,
Well, so it shall be.
J, K, and L,
In peace we will dwell.
M, N, and O,
To play let us go,
P, Q, R, and S,
Love may we possess.
W, X, and Y,

Will not quarrel or die.
Z, and ampersand,
Go to school at command.
Mother Goose rhyme

The real marriage of true minds is for any two people to possess a
sense of humour or irony pitched in exactly the same key, so that their
joint glances at any subject cross like interarching searchlights.
Edith Wharton, A Backward Glance

For the next forty-one years, interrupted only by the quarrels that
would inevitably result between two sensitive egos eager for
acceptance and praise, they were to engage in friendly and familiar
conversation. In Picasso's studio or at the rue de Fleurus, they would
sit, knee to knee—Gertrude [Stein], large and formidable, in her chair;
Picasso, small and intense in his—discussing the personal fortunes and
habits of friends, the difficulties of their own work, their struggles.
James R. Mellow, The Charmed Circle: Gertrude Stein and Company

The most agreeable of all companions is a simple, frank person, without any high pretensions to an oppressive greatness—one who loves life and understands the use of it; obliging alike at all hours; above all, of a golden temper, and steadfast as an anchor. For such an one we gladly exchange the greatest genius, the most brilliant wit, the profoundest thinker.

Gotthold Ephraim Lessing

Friendship is a serious affection; the most sublime of all affections, because it is founded on principle, and cemented by time.

Mary Wollstonecraft

There is no wilderness like a life without friends.

Baltasar Gracián y Morales

We talked as Girls do—
Fond, and late—
We speculated fair, on every subject, but the Grave—
Of ours, none affair—
We handled destinies, as cool—
And we—Disposers—be—

And God, a Quiet Party
To our Authority—
But fondest, dwelt upon Ourself
As we eventual—be—
When Girls to Women, softly raised
We—occupy—Degree—
We parted with a contract
To cherish and to write . . .

Emily Dickinson, from "We Talked as Girls Do"

I want a warm and faithful friend,
to cheer the adverse hour;
Who ne'er to flatter will descend,
nor bend the knee to power.
A friend to chide me when I'm wrong,
my inmost soul to see;
And that my friendship prove as strong
to him as his to me.

John Quincy Adams

I like a Highland friend who will stand by me, not only when I am in the right, but when I am a little in the wrong.
Sir Walter Scott

Yes'm, old friends is always best, 'less you can catch a new one that's fit to make an old one out of.
Sarah Orne Jewett, The Country of the Pointed Firs

Gary Fulcher . . . took great pleasure in teasing Jess about his *"girl* friend." It hardly bothered Jess. He knew that a *girl* friend was somebody who chased you on the playground and tried to grab you and kiss you. He could no more imagine Leslie chasing a boy than he could imagine Mrs. Double-Chinned Myers shinnying up the flagpole.
Katherine Paterson, Bridge to Terabithia

You will cherish friends most if you think of your relation to them as an act of creation and an act of freedom.
Martin E. Marty, Friendship

"Real isn't how you are made," said the Skin Horse. "It's a thing that happens to you. When a child loves you for a long, long time, not just to play with you, but REALLY loves you, then you become Real."

"Does it hurt?" asked the Rabbit.

"Sometimes," said the Skin Horse.

Margery Williams, The Velveteen Rabbit

True love hurts. It always has to hurt. It must be painful to love someone, painful to leave them, you might have to die for them. When people marry they have to give up everything to love each other. The mother who gives birth to her child suffers much. It is the same for us in the religious life. To belong fully to God we have to give up everything. Only then can we truly love. The word "love" is so misunderstood and so misused.

Mother Teresa

Greater love has no one than this, that he lay down his life for his friends.

John 15:13

Tell me who you love and I'll tell you who you are.
Creole proverb

If we would build on a sure foundation in friendship, we must love our friends for their sake rather than for our own.
Charlotte Brontë

Although friendship is a painful task, it is a mistake, I think, to over-emphasize the pain and to forget that payoff is greater than the pain.
Andrew M. Greeley, The Friendship Game

"Good-morning, Christopher Robin," he called out.

"Hallo, Pooh Bear. I can't get this boot on. . . . Do you think you could kindly lean against me, 'cos I keep pulling so hard that I fall over backwards."

Pooh sat down, dug his feet into the ground, and pushed hard against Christopher Robin's back . . . . until he had got [his boot] on.

"And that's that," said Pooh. "What do we do next?"

A. A. Milne, Winnie-the-Pooh

Kindness in words creates confidence. Kindness in thinking creates profoundness. Kindness in giving creates love.

Lao-tse

Life is made up, not of great sacrifices or duties, but of little things, in which smiles and kindness and small obligations win and preserve the heart.

Humphrey Davy

Old friends are best. King James used to call for his old shoes: they were easiest for his feet.

John Selden, Table Talk

I have three chairs in my house: one for solitude, two for friendship, three for company.

Henry Thoreau

Go often to the house of thy friend, for weeds choke the unused path.

Ralph Waldo Emerson

I count that friendship little worth
Which has not many things untold,
Great longings that no words can hold,
And passion-secrets waiting birth.

Along the slender wires of speech
Some message from the heart is sent;
But who can tell the whole that's meant?
Our dearest thoughts are out of reach.

I have not seen thee, though mine eyes
Hold now the image of thy face;
In vain, through form, I strive to trace
The soul I love: that deeper lies.

A thousand accidents control
Our meeting here. Clasp hand in hand,
And swear to meet me in that land
Where friends hold converse soul to soul.

Henry van Dyke, The Upward Path

Times of separation are not a total loss or unprofitable for our companionship, or at any rate they need not be so. In spite of all the difficulties that they bring, they can be the means of strengthening fellowship quite remarkably.

Dietrich Bonhoeffer, letter to Renate and Eberhard Bethge

True friends have no solitary joy or sorrow.

William Ellery Channing

2

The Language of
Friendship

All friendships have the same basic language. Each kindness we show a friend, each way we promote the other, pray for the other, fight for the other's good, welcome the other, thank the other—these are the "words" that form the language of friendship.

Kind words are the music of the world. They have a power which seems to be beyond natural causes, as if they were some angel's song which had lost its way and come on earth. It seems as if they could almost do what in reality God alone can do—soften the hard and angry hearts of men. No one was ever corrected by a sarcasm—crushed, perhaps, if the sarcasm was clever enough, but drawn nearer to God, never.

Frederick William Faber

There is a grace of kind listening, as well as a grace of kind speaking.

Frederick William Faber

Friend . . . GOOD.

Frankenstein monster, in John Whale's The Bride of Frankenstein

One kind word can warm three winter months.

Japanese proverb

It is so gratifying of you to say in your letter that you like me. Things of that kind, which can be very important, people usually omit to mention. Personally, I have no use for unspoken affections, and so I will most readily reply that I like you a great deal.

Sylvia Townsend Warner, letter to Paul Nordoff, 1939

Have you had a kindness shown?
Pass it on!
'Twas not given for thee alone,
Pass it on!
Let it travel down the years,
Let it wipe another's tears, . . .
Pass it on!

Henry Burton

To live is not to live for one's self alone; let us help one another.

Menader of Athens

Dear friends, since God so loved us, we also ought to love one another.

1 John 4:11

To be honest, to be kind—to earn a little and to spend a little less, to make upon the whole a family happier for his presence, to renounce when that shall be necessary and not be embittered, to keep a few friends, but these without capitulation—above all, on the same grim condition, to keep friends with himself—here is a task for all that a man has of fortitude and delicacy.

Robert Louis Stevenson

Kindness is more than deeds. It is an attitude, an expression, a look, a touch. It is anything that lifts another person.

C. Neil Strait

From quiet homes and first beginning,
Out to the undiscovered ends,
There's nothing worth the wear of winning,
But laughter and the love of friends.

Hilaire Belloc

Getters generally don't get happiness; givers get it. You simply give to others a bit of yourself—a thoughtful act, a helpful idea, a word of appreciation, a lift over a rough spot, a sense of understanding, a timely suggestion. You take something out of your mind, garnished in kindness out of your heart, and put it into the other fellow's mind and heart.

Charles H. Burr

The only true knowledge of our fellowman is that which enables us to feel with him . . . which gives us a fine ear for the heart pulses that are beating under the mere clothes of circumstances and opinion.

George Eliot

"The point is, Jeeves, that once more I must pay you a marked tribute."

"Thank you very much, sir."

"Once more you have stepped forward like the great man you are and spread sweetness and light in no uncertain measure."

P. G. Wodehouse, Very Good, Jeeves

My very dear Friend,

May I come near to you now just to let you know that my heart is with you? What else can I say?

George MacDonald

There is a sacredness in tears. They are not the mark of weakness, but of power. They speak more eloquently than ten thousand tongues. They are messengers of overwhelming grief, of deep contrition, and of unspeakable love.

Washington Irving

The verb "to love" in Persian is "to have a friend." "I love you" translated literally is "I have you as a friend," and "I don't like you" simply means "I don't have you as a friend."

Shusha Guppy, The Blindfold Horse: Memories of a Persian Childhood

The story of love is not important—what is important is that one is capable of love. It is perhaps the only glimpse we are permitted of eternity.

Helen Hayes, in Guideposts

Sojourn in every place as if you meant to spend your life there, never omitting an opportunity of doing a kindness, speaking a true word, or making a friend.

John Ruskin

I have found the paradox that if I love until it hurts, then there is no hurt, but only more love.
Mother Teresa

Thin love ain't love at all.
Toni Morrison

Love doesn't just sit there, like a stone; it has to be made, like bread; remade all the time, made new.
Ursula K. Leguin

Love ever gives,
Forgives, outlives,
And ever stands
With open hands.
And while it lives,
It gives.
For this is love's prerogative—
To give, and give, and give.
John Oxenham

How can we thank God enough for you in return for all the joy we have in the presence of our God because of you?

1 Thessalonians 3:9

Love that stammers, that stutters, is apt to be the love that loves best.

Gabriela Mistral

Friendships begun in this world can be taken up again in heaven, never to be broken off.

St. Francis de Sales

And when two people understand each other in their inmost hearts, Their words are sweet and strong, like the fragrance of orchids.

Confucius

Friends are needed both for joy and for sorrow.

Yiddish proverb

An onion with a friend is a roast lamb.

Egyptian proverb

If I don't have friends, then I ain't got nothin'.
Billie Holiday

The highest privilege there is, is the privilege of being allowed to share another's pain. You talk about your pleasures to your acquaintances; you talk about your troubles to your friends.
Fr. Andrew SDC, Seven Words from the Cross

Dear friends, let us love one another, for love comes from God. Everyone who loves has been born of God and knows God.
1 John 4:7

The only thing to do is to hug one's friends tight and do one's job.
Edith Wharton

Do not use a hatchet to remove a fly from your friend's forehead.
Chinese proverb

Friendship is to be purchased only by friendship.
Proverb

And the song, from beginning to end,
I found again in the heart of a friend.
Henry Wadsworth Longfellow

You can imagine Wilbur's surprise when, out of the darkness, came a
small voice he had never heard before. It sounded rather thin, but
pleasant. "Do you want a friend, Wilbur?" it said, "I'll be a friend to
you. I've watched you all day and I like you." . . .
   [When it got light,] Wilbur saw the creature that had spoken to him
in such a kindly way. Stretched across the upper part of the doorway
was a big spiderweb, and hanging from the top of the web, head
down, was a large grey spider. She was about the size of a gumdrop.
E. B. White, Charlotte's Web

Friendship has to be given; no one can take it or demand it or force it.
And for this reason, some have seen friendship a contributor to equality,
Martin E. Marty, Friendship

Joy is a net of love by which you can catch souls.
Mother Teresa

Money buys everything except love, personality, freedom, immortality, silence, peace.

Carl Sandburg

Smiles are as catchin' as the measles and a whole lot more pleasant.

Harvey Hamlyn

For as long as I can remember, I have been playing sports, and for as long as I can remember, my best friends have been my teammates. The camaraderie of the locker room is one of the greatest pleasures.

Sandy Koufax, former Los Angeles Dodgers' pitcher

"Dear Toad, I am glad that you are my best friend.
Your best friend, Frog."

Arnold Lobel, Frog and Toad Are Friends

Cheerfulness is among the most laudable virtues. It gains you the good will and friendship of others. It blesses those who practice it and those upon whom it is bestowed.

B. C. Forbes

Thou wert my guide, philosopher, and friend.
Alexander Pope

In France . . . I was the weekend guest of a couple in their mid-60s who lived a solitary country life, depended mainly on each other for company, and still conversed together with the interest and animation of old friends catching up after a long absence. When I remarked on this, my host said, "To feel really close to another person one must keep a little distance." In other words, we must avoid the aggressive shaping of one person by the other. How seldom we are aware of the tremendous pressure we put on our families and friends to be as we want them to be, rather than the unique person they are. The basic message of human communication is, "Here I am; there you are. We are not alone."
John K. Lagemann

Searching for oneself within is as futile as peeling an onion to find the core: When you finish, there is nothing there but peelings; paradoxically, the only way to find oneself is to go outward to a genuine meeting with another.
Sydney Harris

"Well," said Thelma, "from now on, I will have to be careful when I play with you." "Being careful is not as much fun as being friends," said Frances. "Do you want to be careful or do you want to be friends?"

Russell Hoban, A Bargain for Frances

Girls and boys, come out to play,
The moon doth shine as bright as day;
Leave your supper, and leave your sleep,
And come with your playfellows into the street.
Come with a whoop, come with a call,
Come with a good will or not at all.
Up the ladder and down the wall,
A half-penny roll will serve us all.
You find milk, and I'll find flour,
And we'll have a pudding in half an hour.

Mother Goose rhyme

"Please tame me! . . . If you want a friend, tame me . . ."
    "What must I do, to tame you?" asked the little prince.

"You must be very patient," replied the fox. "First you will sit down at a little distance from me—like that—in the grass. I shall look at you out of the corner of my eye, and you will say nothing. Words are the source of misunderstandings. But you will sit a little closer to me, every day. . . ."

Antoine de Saint-Exupéry, The Little Prince

If you approach each new person in a spirit of adventure, you will find yourself endlessly fascinated by the new channels of thought and experience and personality that you encounter.

Eleanor Roosevelt

Two may talk together under the same roof for many years, yet never really meet; and two others at first speech are old friends.

Mary Catherwood, "Marianson"

If you are old friends, you know all those things about each other and a lot more besides, but they are beside the point. Stripped, humanly speaking, to the bare essentials, you are yourselves the point.

Frederick Buechner, Whistling in the Dark

A real friend is not so much someone you feel free to be serious with as someone you feel free to be silly with.

Sydney J. Harris

The birth of friendship occurs not when one gets a telescope or periscope and starts scanning the horizon of acquaintance or looking above and beyond it. Instead it stands its best chance when there has been a renovation of the person, a move toward becoming open. When the first chink of openness appears in what has once been a closed-circle personality, friendship has a chance. And once it begins its work, more openness follows and the open circle grows. So do the friendships.

Martin E. Marty, Friendship

How much commitment, or covenant, is part of friendship? Does it have to be spoken? Does it have to be declared?

Madeleine L'Engle, "The Meaning of Friendship," Radix

Four things go together: silence, listening, prayer, truth.

Hubert Van Zeller

Friendship of a kind that cannot easily be reversed tomorrow must have its roots in common interests and shared beliefs, and even between nations, in some personal feeling.

Barbara Tuchman, in Harper's Magazine

But after all, the very best thing in good talk, and the thing that helps it most, is *friendship*. How it dissolves the barriers that divide us, and loosens all constraint, and diffuses itself like some fine old cordial through all the veins of life—this feeling that we understand and trust each other, and wish each other heartily well! Everything into which it really comes is good. It transforms letter writing from a task into a pleasure. It makes music a thousand times more sweet. The people who play and sing not *at* us, but *to* us—how delightful it is to listen to them! Yes, there is a talkability that can express itself even without words. There is an exchange of thought and feeling which is happy alike in speech and in silence. It is quietness pervaded with friendship.

Henry van Dyke, The Upward Path

Forgive and forget. The first helps your soul. The second, your liver.

Author unknown

God is the friend of silence. Trees, flowers, grass grow in silence. See the stars, moon, and sun, how they move in silence.

Mother Teresa

He who does not understand your silence will probably not understand your words.

Elbert Green Hubbard

We must listen to our friends, especially when they are not saying much, and be attentive to all expressions of their secret person.

Ignace Lepp, The Ways of Friendship

Blessed is the man who, having nothing to say, abstains from giving in words evidence of the fact.

George Eliot

Conversation is the oldest form of instruction of the human race. It is still an indispensable one. Great books, scientific discoveries, works of art, great perceptions of truth and beauty in any form—all require great conversations to complete their meaning; without it they are abracadabra—color to the blind or music to the deaf. Conversation is the handmaid of learning, true religion and free government. It would be impossible to put too high a price on all we stand to lose by suffering its decay.

A. Whitney Griswold

Friendship arises out of mere Companionship when two or more of the companions discover that they have in common some insight or interest or even taste which the others do not share and which, till that moment, each believed to be his own unique treasure (or burden). The typical expression of opening Friendship would be something like, "What? You too? I thought I was the only one."

C. S. Lewis, The Four Loves

"We must join hands—so," said Anne gravely. "It ought to be over running water. We'll just have to imagine this path is running water. I'll repeat the oath first. I solemnly swear to be faithful to my bosom friend, Diana Barry, as long as the sun and moon shall endure. Now you say it and put my name in."

L. M. Montgomery, Anne of Green Gables

Jonathan said to David, "Go in peace, for we have sworn friendship with each other in the name of the LORD, saying, 'The Lord is witness between you and me, and between your descendants and my descendants forever.'"

1 Samuel 20:42

Pleasant words win many friends, and an affable manner makes acquaintance easy.

Ecclesiasticus 6:5, NEB

He who receives a good turn should never forget it; he who does one should never remember it.

Pierre Charron

I wish my friends to be my friends, and not my masters; to advise me without claiming to control me; to enjoy all kinds of rights over my heart, none over my freedom. . . . Let them always speak to me freely and frankly; they can say anything to me; contempt excepted. I allow them everything.

Jean-Jacques Rousseau, letter to Madame d'Épinay

A friend must not be wounded, even in jest.
Latin proverb

Cover the blemishes and excuse the failings of a friend; draw a curtain before his stains, display his perfection; bury his weakness in silence, proclaim his virtues on the housetop.
Robert South

Write injuries in dust, benefits in marble.
French proverb

One of the finest sides to living is liking people and wanting to share activities in the human enterprise. The greatest pleasures come by giving pleasure to those who work with us, the person who lives next door, and to those who live under the same roof. Entering into this human enterprise, feeling oneself a part of the community, is a very important element which generates happiness.
Fred J. Hafling

What happiness is, no person can say for another. But no one, I am convinced, can be happy who lives only for himself. The joy of living comes from immersion in something that we know to be bigger, better, more enduring and worthier than we are.

John Mason Brown

In the self-help groups that I lead I often hear participants react when someone says, "I just can't seem to move ahead with my life." Others quickly point out improvements they have observed. For example, someone may say, "You are getting better. I remember the first time I met you; all you did was cry. You cried so much that you couldn't even tell us why you were here." Sometimes it takes an outsider to help you see the subtle improvements you have made. Your family and friends may be able to share similar observations.

Helen Fitzgerald, The Mourning Handbook

For one human being to love another: that is perhaps the most difficult of all our tasks; the ultimate, the last test and proof, the work for which all other work is but preparation.

Rainer Maria Rilke

Where deed of mine can help to make this world a better place for men to live in, where word of mine can cheer a despondent heart or brace a weak will, where prayer of mine can serve . . . there let me do and speak and pray.

John Baillie, A Diary of Private Prayer

3

The Shelter of
Friendship

When I get to the *What would I do without so-and-so?* stage of a friendship, two things have happened. My friend has become not only "buddy," but "wonderfriend"—the person who knows exactly what to do when the only word tumbling out of my mouth is "Help!" Also something solid has been created. Our friendship has become a place, a shelter. We have built something together over time.

I feel shelter to speak to you.
Emily Dickinson, letter

A faithful friend is a secure shelter; whoever finds one has found a treasure. A faithful friend is beyond price; his worth is more than money can buy. A faithful friend is an elixir of life, found only by those who fear the Lord.
Ecclesiasticus 6:14-16, NEB

[Friendship] redoubleth joys, and cutteth griefs in halves.
Francis Bacon

Empathy is your pain in my heart.
Jess Lair

It seems to me that trying to live without friends is like milking a bear to get cream for your morning coffee. It is a whole lot of trouble, and then not worth much after you get it.
Zora Neale Hurston, Dust Tracks on a Road

"Jeeves," I said, "I have had occasion to express the view before, and I now express it again fearlessly—you stand in a class of your own."

"Thank you very much, sir. I am glad that everything proceeded satisfactorily."

"The festivities went like a breeze from start to finish. Tell me, were you always like this, or did it come on suddenly?"

"Sir?"

"The brain. The grey matter. Were you an outstandingly brilliant boy?"

"My mother thought me intelligent, sir."

P. G. Wodehouse, Very Good, Jeeves

All of a sudden Chauntecleer felt profoundly sorry for Chauntecleer.

"Well, they rot!" he decided with monumental dignity. "I can do without them. . . . Let them go their selfish ways. Chauntecleer the Rooster was ever the noblest bird of them all!" And speaking that way in his heart, Chauntecleer composed himself for an eternity of lonely suffering.

But the colors around him never stopped pulsing. . . . They were taking form. . . . The shape was the shape of a Cow.

Chauntecleer's heart leaped! . . . "You didn't forget!" Chauntecleer cried—without opening his mouth. "You saw my suffering! They left me but you, my friend—you came back to me!"

Walter Wangerin, Jr., The Book of the Dun Cow

In short I will part with anything for you but you.

Lady Mary Wortley Montagu

My brightest spot, next to my love of *old* friends, is the deliciously calm *new* friendship that Herbert Spencer gives me. We see each other every day, and have a delightful *camaraderie* in everything. But for him my life would be desolate enough. What a wretched lot of old shrivelled creatures we shall be by-and-by. Never mind—the uglier we get in the eyes of others, the lovelier we shall be to each other; that has always been my firm faith about friendship, and now it is in a slight degree my experience.

George Eliot, letter to Miss Sara Hennell

My life will be sour grapes and ashes without you.

Daisy Ashford (age 9), The Young Visitors

Do not forget me; you see that I do not forget you. It is pleasing in the silence of solitude to think, that there is one at least, however distant, of whose benevolence there is little doubt, and whom there is yet hope of seeing again.

Samuel Johnson, letter to Bennet Langton

Lookee here, Pip, at what is said to you by a true friend. Which this to you the true friend say. If you can't get to be oncommon through going straight, you'll never get to do it through going crooked. So don't tell me no more on 'em, Pip, and live well and die happy.

Charles Dickens, Great Expectations

Hand grasps hand, eye lights eye in good friendship,
And great hearts expand
And grow in the sense of this world's life.

Ralph Waldo Emerson

We love those who know the worst of us and don't turn their faces away.

Walker Percy

Oh the comfort, the inexpressible comfort of feeling safe with a person: having neither to weigh thoughts nor measure words, but to pour them out. Just as they are—chaff and grain together, knowing that a faithful hand will take and sift them, keep what is worth keeping, and then with the breath of kindness, blow the rest away.
George Eliot

"Why, what's happened to your tail?" [Pooh] said in surprise. . . .

"Somebody must have taken it," said Eeyore. "How like them," he added, after a long silence.

Pooh felt he ought to say something helpful about it, but didn't quite know what. So he decided to do something helpful instead.

"Eeyore," he said solemnly, "I, Winnie-the-Pooh, will find your tail for you."

"Thank you, Pooh," answered Eeyore. "You're a real friend," said he. "Not like some," he said.
A. A. Milne, Winnie-the-Pooh

Your truest friends are those who visit you in prison or in the hospital.
Moroccan proverb

Friendship is unnecessary, like philosophy, like art. It has no survival value; rather it is one of those things that give value to survival.

C. S. Lewis

Hold a true friend with both your hands.

Nigerian proverb

I think you must know without my putting it into words (for I cannot) how deep such friendship and support goes with me and how large a part it constitutes of such strength as I have in public affairs. I thank you with all my heart and with deep affection.

Woodrow Wilson to Edward M. House

Few delights can equal the mere presence of one whom we trust utterly.

George MacDonald

Such is friendship that through it we love places and seasons; for as bright bodies emit rays to a distance, and flowers drop their sweet leaves on the ground around them, so friends impart favor even to the places where they dwell. With friends even poverty is pleasant. Words cannot express the joy which a friend imparts; they only can know who have experienced that joy. A friend is dearer than the light of heaven, for it would be better for us that the sun were extinguished than that we should be without friends.

Chrysostom

Love comforteth like sunshine after rain.

William Shakespeare

The feeling of friendship is like that of being comfortably filled with roast beef.

Samuel Johnson

Two are better than one, because they have a good return for their work: If one falls down, his friend can help him up. But pity the man who falls and has no one to help him up!

Ecclesiastes 4:9-10

We are born helpless. As soon as we are fully conscious we discover loneliness. We need others physically, emotionally, intellectually. We

need them if we are to know anything, even ourselves.
C. S. Lewis

No one is so rich that he does not need another's help; no one so poor as not to be useful in some way to his fellow man.
Pope Leo XIII

A Lion was sleeping in his lair, when a Mouse, not knowing where he was going, ran over the mighty beast's nose and awakened him. The Lion clapped his paw upon the frightened little creature, and was about to make an end of him in a moment, when the Mouse, in pitiable tone, besought him to spare one who had so unconsciously offended, and not stain his honourable paws with so insignificant a prey. The Lion, smiling at his little prisoner's fright, generously let him go.

Now it happened no long time after, that the Lion, while ranging the woods for his prey, fell into the toils of the hunters; and finding himself entangled without hope of escape, set up a roar that filled the whole forest with its echo. The Mouse, recognising the voice of his former preserver, ran to the spot, and without more ado set to work to nibble the knot in the cord that bound the Lion, and in a short time set the noble beast at liberty; thus convincing him that kindness is seldom thrown away, and that there is no other creature so much below another but that he may have it in his power to return a good office.

Aesop's Fables

If you have but a solitary friend, who is tried and true, you are among the rich in mind and heart. You then have an investment that never loses its value. You will grow richer each day of your life. Once you have that kind of friendship, do not expect too much of it. Measure it out. Give to it all the loyalty that is yours, and what a possession you will then have!

George Matthew Adams

When the heart is full, the eyes overflow.

Shalom Aleichem

Better to have a hundred friends than a hundred rubles.

Russian proverb

By friendship you mean the greatest love, the greatest usefulness, the most open communication, the noblest sufferings, the severest truth, the heartiest counsel, and the greatest union of minds of which brave men and women are capable.

Jeremy Taylor

There are not many things in life so beautiful as true friendship, and there are not many things more uncommon.

Megiddo message

Rejoice with those who rejoice; mourn with those who mourn.

Romans 12:15

Home is not where you live but where they understand you.

Christian Morgenstern

Happiness is not so much in having as sharing. We make a living by what we get, but we make a life by what we give.

Norman MacEwan

While such friends are near us we feel that all is well. Perhaps we never saw them before and they may never cross our life's path again; but the influence of their calm, mellow natures is a libation poured upon our discontent, and we feel its healing touch as the ocean feels the mountain stream freshening its brine.

Helen Keller

If we would build on a sure foundation in friendship, we must love our friends for their sakes rather than our own.

Charlotte Brontë

A despairing man should have the devotion of his friends.

Job 6:14

Nothing can fill the gap when we are away from those we love, and it would be wrong to try and find anything. We must simply hold out and win through. That sounds very hard at first, but at the same time it is a great consolation, since leaving the gap unfilled preserves the bond between us. It is nonsense to say that God fills the gap; he does not fill it, but keeps it empty so that our communion with one another may be kept alive, even at the cost of pain.

Dietrich Bonhoeffer

It is a glorious privilege to live, to know, to act, to listen, to behold, to love. To look up at the blue summer sky; to see the sun sink slowly beyond the line of the horizon; to watch the worlds come twinkling into view, first one by one, and the myriads that no man can count, and lo! the universe is white with them; and you and I are here.

Marco Morrow

Love is always building up. It puts some line of beauty on every life it touches. It gives new hope to discouraged ones, new strength to those who are weak. It helps the despairing to rise and start again. It makes life seem more worthwhile to everyone into whose eyes it looks. Its words are benedictions. Its every breath is full of inspiration.

Author unknown

To friendship every burden is light.

Proverb

Now friendship possesses many splendid advantages, but of course the finest thing of all about it is that it sends a ray of good hope into the future, and keeps our hearts from faltering or falling by the wayside.

Aristotle

Saul and Jonathan—
in life they were loved and gracious,
and in death they were not parted.

2 Samuel 1:23

Holy Friendship that has medicine for all the wretchedness is not to be despised. From God it truly is, that amid the wretchedness of this exile, we be comforted with the counsel of friends until we come to Him.

Richard Rolle, The Fire of Love, Bk. 2

[When you are grieving] you may want to talk to someone who has traveled his or her grief journey a few miles ahead of you. It really helps to know you are not alone, not "crazy," and not a failure. And if you have misplaced yours for awhile, borrow hope from a friend.

Sandra L. Graves, in What to Do When a Loved One Dies

No medicine is more valuable, none more efficacious, none better suited to the cure of all our temporal ills than a friend to whom we may turn for consolation in time of trouble—and with whom we may share our happiness in time of joy.

St. Aelred of Rievaulx, Christian Friendship

Let me not to the marriage of true minds
Admit impediments. Love is not love
Which alters when it alteration finds,
Or bends with the remover to remove.
O no, it is an ever-fix'ed mark
That looks on tempests and is never shaken,
It is the star to every wand'ring bark. . . .

William Shakespeare, "Sonnet 116"

Loneliness is the first thing which God named not good.

John Milton

I was free; but there was no one to welcome me to the land of freedom. I was a stranger in a strange land, and my home after all was down in the old cabin quarter, with the old folks, and my brothers and sisters. But to this solemn resolution I came; I was free, and they should be free also; I would make a home for them in the North, and the Lord helping me, I would bring them all there. Oh, how I prayed then, lying all alone on the cold, damp ground: "Oh, dear Lord," I said, "I ain't got no friend but you. Come to my help, Lord, for I'm in trouble!"

Harriet Tubman

Joys divided are increased.

John G. Holland

[Piglet] gave a very long sigh and said, "I wish Pooh were here. It's so much more friendly with two."

A. A. Milne, Winnie-the-Pooh

The person who tries to live alone will not succeed as a human being. His heart withers if it does not answer another heart. His mind shrinks away if he hears only the echoes of his own thoughts and finds no other inspiration.

Pearl S. Buck

How sweet, how passing sweet is solitude!
But grant me still a friend in my retreat,
Whom I may whisper, solitude is sweet.
William Cowper, "Retirement"

Robbing life of friendship is like robbing the world of the sun.
Cicero

It is great to have friends when one is young, but indeed it is still
more so when you are getting old. When we are young, friends are,
like everything else, a matter of course. In the old days we know what
it means to have them.
Edvard Grieg

"I need all the friends I can get."
Charlie Brown, Peanuts

There was another fellow in our room who just loved those
caterpillars. . . . Every day he would literally wrap himself around the
[caterpillar] jar and hug it until I could persuade him to try another

activity. He simply loved those caterpillars. Some days his "friends" as he called them, would stay on his desk throughout the school day.

Susan Klein, "Willie the Bug-Man," Best-Loved Stories Told at the National Storytelling Festival

Once I found a friend. "Dear me," I said, "he was made for me." But now I find more and more friends who seem to have been made for me, and more and yet more made for me. Is it possible we were all made for each other all over the world?

G. K. Chesterton

We are all travellers in the wilderness of this world, and the best that we find in our travels is an honest friend.

Samuel Johnson

"Do you know what we need?" Leslie called to him. Intoxicated as he was with the heavens, he couldn't imagine needing anything on earth. "We need a place," she said, "just for us. It would be so secret that we would never tell anyone in the whole world about it. . . . It might be a secret country," she continued, "and you and I would be the rulers of it."

Katherine Paterson, Bridge to Terabithia

For the ease with which I passed the year, I was, however, somewhat indebted to the society of my fellow-slaves. They were noble souls; they not only possessed loving hearts, but brave ones. We were linked and interlinked with each other. I loved them with a love stronger than any thing I have experienced since. . . . I believe we would have died for each other. We never undertook to do any thing, of any importance, without a mutual consultation. We never moved separately. We were one; and as much so by our tempers and dispositions, as by the mutual hardships to which we were necessarily subjected by our condition as slaves.

Frederick Douglass

A faithful friend is an image of God.

French proverb

Thank you, too, dear Susie, that you never weary of me, or never *tell* me so, and that when the world is cold, and the storm sighs e'er so piteously, I am sure of one sweet shelter, *one* covert from the storm!

Emily Dickinson, letter to Susan Gilbert (Dickinson)

In all my life, until I met you, I never had a friend.

Tom Wolfe, a fragment written in his journal but never sent to his friend Max Perkins

My heart's dear pleasure, bless you for your kind long friendship. I hope I haven't been a great pest.

John Masefield

4

The Grace of Friendship

It's often in the lonely moments—when friends are oceans, worlds, latitudes and longitudes away—that we appreciate friendship as one of God's great gifts to us, the hand of God holding us up through the hand of a friend.

Who can adequately marvel at the grace gift of friendship? To have someone who gives and forgives when it's undeserved; who doesn't condemn when it is deserved. This is a mystery, grace upon grace.

To be glad of life, because it gives you the chance to love and to work and to play and to look up at the stars; to be contented with your possessions, but not satisfied with yourself until you have made the best of them; to despise nothing in the world except falsehood and meanness, and to fear nothing except cowardice; to be governed by your admirations rather than by your disgusts; to covet nothing that is your neighbor's except his kindness of heart and gentleness of manners: to think seldom of your enemies, often of your friends, and every day of Christ; and to spend as much time as you can, with body and with spirit, in God's out-of-doors—these are little guideposts on the footpath to peace.

Henry van Dyke, The Upward Path

I awoke this morning with devout thanksgiving for my friends, the old and the new. Shall I not call God the Beautiful, who daily showeth himself to me in his gifts?

Ralph Waldo Emerson

Friendship is . . . a *gift.* Indeed, it is essentially and primarily a gift.

Andrew M. Greeley, The Friendship Game

When men are friendly, even water is sweet.
Chinese proverb

All my prayers for you are full of praise to God! When I pray for you, my heart is full of joy . . .
Philippians 1:3, TLB

What a thing friendship is, world without end!
Robert Browning

A multitude of small delights constitutes happiness.
Charles Baudelaire

The collected pleasures of everyday life fade away quickly unless there is at the heart of them the gladness of having done something that has made someone happier.
Author unknown

Shared joy is double joy, and shared sorrow is half-sorrow.
Swedish proverb

I count myself in nothing else so happy
As in a soul remembering my good friends.
William Shakespeare

Friendship improves happiness, and abates misery, by doubling our joy,
and dividing our grief.
Joseph Addison

Friendship breeds a mutual delight.
Charles H. Spurgeon, "Friendship"

Love stretches your heart and makes you big inside.
Margaret Walker

For there is nothing more productive of joy than the repayment of
kindness, or the sharing of interests and exchange of favors.
Cicero, On Friendship, *translated by Frank O. Copley*

Blessed are they who have the gift of making friends, for it is one of
God's best gifts. It involves many things, but above all, the power of

going out of one's self and appreciating whatever is noble and loving in another.

Thomas Hughes

One can pay back the loan of gold, but one lies forever in debt to those who are kind.

Malay proverb

The glory of friendship is not the outstretched hand, nor the kindly smile nor the joy of companionship; it is the spirited inspiration that comes to one when he discovers that someone else believes in him and is willing to trust him.

Ralph Walso Emerson

Cheerful company shortens the miles.

German proverb

Real friends are those who, when you've made a fool of yourself, don't feel that you've done a permanent job.

Erwin T. Randall

How good and pleasant it is when brothers live together in unity!
It is like precious oil poured on the head, running down on the beard. . . .
It is as if the dew of Hermon were falling on Mount Zion.

Psalm 133

Sure the world is full of trouble, but as long as we have people
undoing trouble, we have a pretty good world.

Helen Keller

If instead of a gem, or even a flower, we should cast the gift of a
loving thought into the heart of a friend; that would be giving as the
angels give.

George MacDonald

To a friend's house the road is never long.

Dutch proverb

The impulse of love that leads us to the doorway of a friend is the
voice of God within.

Agnes Sanford

I never tired of Helen Burns; nor ever ceased to cherish for her a sentiment of attachment, as strong, tender, and respectful as any that ever animated my heart. How could it be otherwise, when Helen, at all times and under all circumstances, evinced for me a quiet and faithful friendship, which ill-humour never soured nor irritation ever troubled?

Charlotte Brontë, Jane Eyre

The world is so empty if one thinks only of mountains, rivers, and cities; but to know someone here and there who thinks and feels with us, and who, though distant, is close to us in spirit, this makes the earth an inhabited garden.

Goethe

The meeting of two personalities is like the contact of two chemical substances; if there is any reaction, both are transformed.

Carl Jung

In friendship we discover and reveal what we are and, perhaps still more, what we are capable of becoming.

Ignace Lepp, The Ways of Friendship

The people who can share a woman's feelings best are other women. Because . . . they have been there. Some friends are forever. Some are for the moment. Both are to be treasured.

Lynn Caine, Lifelines

I've dreamed of meeting her all my life . . . a bosom friend—an intimate friend, you know—a really kindred spirit to whom I can confide my inmost soul.

L. M. Montgomery, Anne of Green Gables

A true friend is a forever friend.

George MacDonald

How often you and I
Had tired the sun with talking.

William Cory, from "Heraclitus"

It is the heart that makes a man rich. He is rich according to what he is, not according to what he has.

Henry Ward Beecher

It's good to have money and the things that money can buy, but it's good, too, to check up once in a while and make sure you haven't lost the things that money can't buy.

George Horace Lorimer

My friend, the things that do attain
The happy life be these, I find;
The riches left, not got with pain;
The fruitful ground, the quiet mind;
The equal friend; no grudge, no strife;
No charge of rule, nor governance;
Without disease the healthy life;
The household of continuance.

Henry Howard, Earl of Surrey

O grant me, Heaven, a middle state,
Neither too humble nor too great;
More than enough, for nature's ends,
With something left to treat my friends.

David Mallet

Many spirits might have failed beneath the bitterness of their trial had they not found a friend.

Charles H. Spurgeon, "Friendship"

Be kind; everyone you meet is fighting a hard battle.

John Watson

One loving heart sets another on fire.

Augustine

One of the best of men said to me once that he did not feel any longing after immortality, but, when he thought of certain persons, he could not for a moment believe they had ceased. He had beheld the lovely, believed therefore in the endless.

George MacDonald

The fingers of God touch a life when you touch a friend.

Mary Dawn Hughes

There are many kinds of love, as many kinds of light,

And every kind of love makes a glory in the night.
There is love that stirs the heart, and love that gives it rest,
But the love that leads life upward is the noblest and the best.
Henry van Dyke, The Upward Path

The older I grow in years, the more the wonder and the joy increase when I see the power of these words of Jesus—"I have called you friends"—to move the human heart. That one word "friend" breaks down each barrier of reserve.
Charles F. Andrews

The very possibility of friendship with God transfigures life. The religious convictions, thus, tend inevitably to deepen every human friendship, to make it vastly more significant.
Henry Churchill King, The Laws of Friendship

In the midst of lonely days and dreary nights I have heard an inner voice saying, "Lo, I will be with you."
Martin Luther King, Jr.

There is no shop anywhere where one can buy friendship.
Antoine de Saint-Exupéry, The Little Prince

He loseth nothing that keepeth God for his friend.
Thomas Fuller, Gnomologia: Adages and Proverbs

I love you for putting your hand into my heaped-up heart, and passing over all the foolish and weak things, and for drawing out into the light all the beautiful and radiant qualities that no one else has looked quite deep enough to find.
Anonymous

A true friend unbosoms freely, advises justly, assists readily, adventures boldly, takes all patiently, defends courageously, and continues a friend unchangeable.
William Penn

No burden is too heavy when it is carried with love.
Anonymous

Friendship is a miracle by which a person consents to view from a certain distance, and without coming any nearer, the very being who is necessary to him as food.

Simone Weil

If You care for me
speak to me without words
in a spiral of starlings
thrown into a bank of wind, scarves
of an invisible dancer
making the sky a stage. . . .

Luci Shaw, "If you care for me," Polishing the Petoskey Stone

Sometimes I must pause in amazement: To think of all the things we have been through, and what a miracle that we have survived it all up to this point!

Letter from Thomas Mann to Erich Kahler, translation by Richard and Clara Winston

Friendship is love with understanding.

Ancient proverb

It is only necessary to know that love is a direction and not a state of the soul. If one is unaware of this, one falls into despair at the first onslaught of affliction.

Simone Weil

Love is a fruit in season at all times, and within reach of every hand. Anyone may gather it and no limit is set. Everyone can reach this love through meditation, spirit of prayer, and sacrifice, by an intense inner life.

Mother Teresa

People come into our lives to teach us, and each person is a special gift to be treasured and never taken for granted. Some people seem to be placed into our lives as comforters who help us to get through: special friends, resource people, family members who weren't close or available before.

Catherine M. Sanders, Surviving Grief . . . and Learning to Live Again

The thread of our life would be dark, Heaven knows, if it were not with friendship and love interwin'd.

Thomas Moore

You can kiss your family and friends good-bye and put miles between you, but at the same time you carry them with you in your heart, your mind, your stomach, because you do not just live in a world but a world lives in you.

Frederick Buechner

Whether or not I find the missing thing
it will always be
more than my thought of it.
Silver-heavy, somewhere it winks
in its own small privacy
playing
the waiting game with me.

And the real treasures do not vanish.
The precious loses no value
in the spending.
A piece of hope spins out
bright, along the dark, and is not

lost in space;
verity is a burning boomerang;
love is out orbiting and will
come home.

Luci Shaw, "But not forgotten," Listen to the Green

No, we need not forget our dear loved ones; but we may cling forever to the enduring hope that there will be a time when we can meet unfettered and be blessed in that land of everlasting sun where the soul drinks from the living streams of love that roll by God's high throne.

Dwight L. Moody, Heaven

Let me remember now my friends with love and my enemies with forgiveness, entrusting them all . . . to Thy protecting care. . . . Amen.

John Baillie, A Diary of Private Prayer

[Prayer] holds all the other things we have in common together.

Luci Shaw, "The Meaning of Friendship," Radix

Christ be with me, Christ be within me,
Christ behind me, Christ before me, . . .
Christ in hearts of all that love me,
Christ in mouth of friend and stranger.

St. Patrick